IMAGES
of America

KENNEBUNKPORT

IMAGES
of America

KENNEBUNKPORT

Compiled by
Connie Porter Scott

ARCADIA
PUBLISHING

Published by Arcadia Publishing
Charleston, South Carolina

For all general information contact Arcadia Publishing at:
Telephone 843-853-2070
Fax 843-853-0044
E-mail sales@arcadiapublishing.com
For customer service and orders:
Toll-Free 1-888-313-2665

Visit us on the Internet at www.arcadiapublishing.com

Contents

Dedicated
To Nana
With Love

Goldie Perry Huff
1893–1993

When asked to gather materials and write this book on Kennebunkport, I couldn't believe my good fortune. My next thought was, "Oh, Nana, you've gone when I need you most!"

Goldie Perry Huff was born and lived in Cape Porpoise all her life. She either knew or knew of the members of most of the families who ever crossed the bridge to the Cape or Port. Growing up close by, I was forever hearing the ancestral litany of Great Aunt Nell, cousin to what's-her-name who married you-know, and so on. And like most young people, I'd politely nod while wondering, perhaps, how I'd spend my nickel at Carl and Lois's or if she'd take me swimming that day in the Cove.

So here I am in 1994, just a year after her passing, presenting a pictorial record of all those places and people she so often spoke of and that, as a result, have become so much a part of me.

For this belated appreciation of my heritage and for those roots she planted and nurtured that have literally opened doors into other's homes and albums, Nana, I thank you. I couldn't have done this without you. And I hope this book, in some small way, makes up for all those not-so-polite nods.

Connie

OLDE GRIST MILL 1749–1994 (see page 128).

Introduction

Though starting an introduction with a negative may not, in a literary sense, be the best approach, I feel compelled to begin with what this book is not. It is not a history of Kennebunkport. You will not find the wreck of the *Wandby* or the sinking of the *Isadore* here. As a history, the absence of those events from these pages, along with other worthy people and places, would be regrettable, if not unforgivable. That said, let's focus on what this book is.

The Images of America Series: Kennebunkport is a nostalgic journey into yesteryear with emphasis on the area's people and places, many of whom are no longer with us. My involvement and enthusiasm for this project comes from my background as a writer and my ancestry. I grew up in Kennebunkport/Cape Porpoise listening to my great-great-grandparents, grandparents, and assorted aunts and cousins discuss the people, places, and events that made up everyday life. I skated at the Mill Pond, went to the movies at the theater in Dock Square, and worked one summer at the Langsford House. My roots are deep; my memories are vivid and, with great affection, this will always be my hometown.

In gathering and presenting materials for this book, I strove to preserve my memories and those of others, and to put faces to names for both present and future generations. Within that context, this endeavor may be said to have "historical significance," though it is not a history in a scholarly sense.

Materials within these pages are arranged chronologically, as best as possible, rather than by subject matter. By the time I realized the danger I was in—where to place a photograph taken "about" 1910 or *c.* 1909—I had worked through the shipbuilding era and was on my way by trolley to the Casino at the Cape; it was too late to turn back. My hope is that the visual progression through the decades imparts a "feeling" of years passing by and an eagerness to see what the next decade will bring.

Some of the photographs in this book will be familiar to those living in the area who have remarkable collections of their own. Other photographs have been languishing in tucked-away family albums and have never before been in print. Hopefully, these photographs will both surprise and delight those who have only heard about the Doughnut Gang, night mackerel fishing, or the Christmas triplets.

Our photo/journey begins in the 1800s and takes us through the 1940s and into the '50s. Along the way you'll meet Pharaoh Perry, Ernest Benson, and Captain Frank Nunan himself, with a brief stop at the Shiloh Hotel and the Ocean Bluff.

Hope you enjoy the trip.

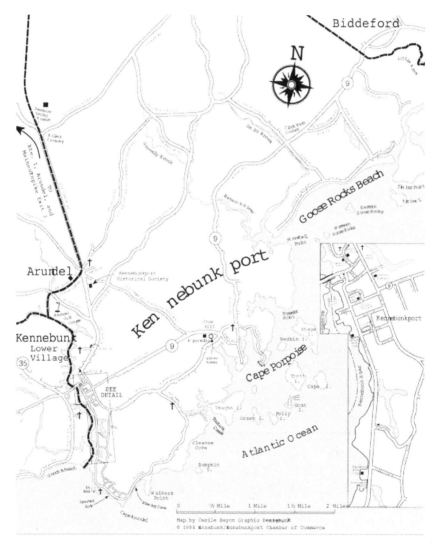

One

1800–1899

GRANITE QUARRY. James Edward Coburn Sr. of Biddeford sits atop a granite block taken from one of several quarries in the Kennebunkport area in the 1830s where the stone was rated "superior." James's daughter, Mary, married Harrison Huff and lived on the Langsford Road, Cape Porpoise. A religious woman, she was baptised in the ocean off the shores of the Langsford House. (Huff Family)

OUT ON THE TIDE. A three-masted schooner is guided through the locks on the Kennebunk River in the mid-1800s. The 16-foot-high walls were built from Kennebunkport granite and helped raise the water level so large ships could float through at high tide. (Kenneth Hutchins Family)

BUSY RIVER. Boat houses, coal sheds, and wharves dot the shores of the Kennebunk River during its heyday of boat building in the mid to latter part of the nineteenth century. The West India route proved a lucrative market in the mid-century and Boston investors were attracted to the Kennebunk River boatyards where quality vessels were being turned out at wages of about $1.50 per day. (Gloria Rand Sundin)

10

THE PIER. The Shiloh Hotel at left, Goat Island Light in the distance, and Pinkham's Wharf on Bickford Island, now the Pier, as they were in the 1880s. From these shores crews tended the schooners of the famous Nunan fishing fleet which sailed from its harbor. The island is attached by a causeway to the mainland, known as Cape Porpoise. (Huff Family)

SHILOH HOTEL. An ocean view from every room, along with boating and bathing, attracted guests to the Shiloh Hotel on Bickford Island in the early 1880s. It was later sold and renamed the Waban. It burned in 1887. (Huff Family)

LORD MANSION. Many of the area's wealthier citizens and businessmen resided at the Port, then called Arundel, including Nathaniel Lord, a merchant and shipbuilder. During the War of 1812 he made use of unemployed shipbuilders and erected a mansion with thirty-six rooms, corresponding with his age at the time. Overlooking Ocean Avenue, the Captain Lord Mansion is presently operated as an inn by Rick Litchfield and was named to the National Register of Historic Places in 1973. A child's rocking horse can be seen in this 1847 print from a daguerrotype taken when the mansion was occupied by Nathanial's widow Phebe and eldest son, Daniel, and family. A spiral staircase leading to the rooftop cupola once had an outside entrance "so that villagers could climb to view inbound ships and not disturb the residents of the mansion." (Rick Litchfield Print)

NORTON HOUSE. Built in 1893 by R.W. Norton and located in the square overlooking the river, the three-story hotel was lost to fire in the early 1900s. (Kenneth Hutchins Family)

PARKER HOUSE. A summer hotel built in 1878 on the site of the present post office, the luxurious Parker House featured three floors to accommodate 150 guests, a large dance hall and music room, a veranda with a view, and a stable with carriages and dog carts. It was dismantled in the 1930s and the bathroom fixtures were offered to area residents, many of whom still lacked indoor plumbing. (Kenneth Hutchins Family)

SPRING HOTEL. One of the earliest hotels at the Port was the Spring House on Elm Street, owned by George Malings when it burned in "the skating rink fire" of 1887. (Kenneth Hutchins Family)

MALINGS. In this family group are, from left to right: (front) Israel and Irene; (second row) Ida, Thomas, Mary (Mother), and Ted; (back) Henry, Robert, John, William, and Charles. The Malings owned and operated the Spring Hotel on Elm Street, Kennebunkport, *c.* 1880. (Bunty Lush)

STONE HAVEN. On the far right is the Stone Haven Hotel, built by Thomas G. Stone in the mid-1800s onto the ell seen in back. To the left were summer cottages, and to the left of the cottages was the building known as the Stone Haven Annex, built in 1905. The Stone Haven, and later the Annex, were among the area's most popular summer hotels. The Stone Haven burned in 1931. The Annex is also gone. (Huff Family)

GARRISON HOUSE. Located at the head of the Cove on the Pier Road at the Cape, the Garrison House may well be the oldest house in Kennebunkport. This post card dates it to 1722, about the same time the Tristram Perkins III House on Oak Street was built, though the date of record for the Garrison House is 1730. It was built by the Reverend Thomas Prentice and is now an inn, owned and operated by Lyman and Louise Huff. (Huff Collection)

15

OCEAN BLUFF. This imposing 200-by-50 foot hotel was built in 1873 by the Kennebunkport Seashore Co. off Ocean Avenue where the Colony is now located. It was destroyed by fire in 1902. (Kenneth Hutchins Family)

ASHES AND RUBBLE. Above are the remains of the Ocean Bluff after the devastating fire. A new hotel, Breakwater Court, was eventually built on the site by R.W. Norton, owner of the Norton House that burned. (Kenneth Hutchins Family)

PERKINS-NOTT. This majestic, white-columned mansion on Spring Street was built in 1853 by Eliphalet Perkins III, a descendant of one of the area's earliest families. He sold it to his son, Charles, who moved in that year with his new bride, Celia Nott. The newlyweds spared no expense in decorating and furnishing their home and many of the original pieces remain. The mansion was left to the Kennebunkport Historical Society in 1955 and is open to visitors. (Bunty Lush)

STONE MANSION. Built by the Reverend Edward Clark in 1822, the Stone Mansion stood where Port Gardens is now located on Ocean Avenue. The salt water rocks were shipped from one of the islands. (Huff Family)

CAPE PORPOISE SQUARE. (Carolyn Craig)

B.U. HUFF. Benjamin Huff, along with S.H. Pinkham, both of Cape Porpoise, were listed among the leading businessmen of the late 1800s. Benjamin operated a grocery store in the white building farthest to the right in the photograph on the right. This is the same building that for a short time housed the primary school (see page 26). (Huff Family)

PERRYS. William II and Jane Hutchins Perry stand at the entrance to their home on the Langsford Road, Cape Porpoise, in the late 1800s. William, a Civil War veteran, purchased the house from Benjamin U. Huff who built it in 1870. Jane's father, Asa, was lost at sea in 1842, leaving six daughters. She was the youngest. (Huff Family)

HIGH FASHION. Four women of the Cape sit for a formal photograph, *c.* 1890. Clockwise, from front: Caroline Jennison Moody, Lettina Ghen Perry, unknown, and Lillian Huff. (Huff Family)

TRIPLETS. Christmas came in three's in 1868 when Mrs. John E. Seavey of Cape Porpoise gave birth to triplets on Christmas Day. From left to right, at about age 3: Minnie, Kittie, and Carrie. All three married—Minnie to Thomas Cluff, two children; Kittie to Henry Dennett, no children; and Carrie to Dana Cluff, twelve children. (Dana & Marie Campbell)

SUNDAY BEST. Ladies at the Cape in Sunday finery, *c.* 1900. From left to right are: Lillian Huff, EstherWoods,AlbertinaLapierre, Grace Stinson, and Sadie Nunan. (Fred & Harriett Eaton)

BELL & FLETCHER'S. Luman Fletcher, left, and William Perry II tend the horses at the livery stable on the Langsford Road, across the street from the Perry home, c. 1890. Horses and carriages were available to rent (see price list below) or horses could be boarded. (Huff Family).

Bell & Fletcher's Stable
PRICE LIST.

TO	7 Passenger Buckboard	9 Passenger Buckboard
Kennebunk Port	$ 3.50	$ 4.50
Kennebunk Beach	5.25	6.75
Kennebunk Village	5.25	6.75
Parsons Beach	7.00	9.00
Beachwood	3.50	4.50
Ocean Bluff	5.25	6.75
Hills Beach	7.00	9.00
Biddeford or Saco	7.00	9.00
Mousam Falls	8.75	11.25
Biddeford Pool	7.00	9.00
Old Orchard Beach	10.50	13.50
Bald Head Cliff	10.50	13.50
Fortunes Rocks	5.25	6.75
York Harbor*	12.00	15.00

*One dollar extra will be charged to drive in to Bald Head Cliff.

BELL & FLETCHER PRICE LIST.

BLACKSMITHS. Horses were an integral part of daily life in the early twentieth century and the area supported several livery stables and blacksmith shops. Will Jennison's blacksmith shop at the Cape, seen above, was built in 1899 and located in the square next to the school at far right. (Kenneth Hutchins Family)

SMITHY. Benson's blacksmith shop at the Port did business on the corner of Temple and Maine Streets. (Harrison Seavey)

DOCK SQUARE. In this *c.* 1900 photograph, a driver stops his horse and buggy at the weighing scale in the square, prior to the Soldier's Monument being built. To the right is a fountain, and to the left a road leads to the Perkins' coal sheds on the Kennebunk River. (Harrison Seavey)

POST OFFICE SQUARE. A downtown street scene of the square, which was named for the post office located there at the turn of the century. (Kenneth Hutchins Family)

CANOE RACES. Recreation on the Kennebunk River included canoe races and picnicking at the turn of the century, coinciding with high and low tides. (George Bush Family album)

GALA. Residents and vacationers join in the festivities on the Kennebunk River, scene of the annual River Carnival and weekend outings. (Kenneth Hutchins Family)

ETHELRED MILL. Built in 1877, this mill turned out shingles and lathes. It was located on the Mills Road in Cape Porpoise, on what now is the Preble property. (Luverne Clough Preble)

TRANQUIL. Print on the roof of the Olde Grist Mill, at left, reads, "Corn, Flour, Oats, Meal & shorts, For Sale by, J.D. Perkins." This town landmark on Mill Lane was the last of the U.S. tidal mills. In back of the mill today is a gift shop, once the boat house of Clement Clark, who was a grand nephew of noted shipbuilder David Clark (see page 128). (Luverne Clough Preble)

CLUFF'S. Four of Dana and (triplet) Carrie Cluff's twelve children are, from left to right: John, Vira, Robert, and Harold, c. 1900. (Dana & Marie Campbell)

CROW HILL. Carrie and Enoch Curtis head up Crow Hill, Cape Porpoise, where their home was located in the late 1800s. Some neighbors, preferring a more genteel address, claimed "Cape Porpoise Highlands" as their residence instead of Crow Hill, but the name never stuck. To their left was the Prospect House, a small summer hotel "only about four hours' ride from Boston." The Curtis house was lost in the 1947 fires. (Huff Family)

CAPE SCHOOL 1872. Primary school was temporarily held here in Benjamin U. Huff's store before the new school was built in the square. Identification was provided with the old tintype. From left to right are: (front row) Arthur Hutchins, George Stone, Albert Hutchins, and James Simmons Holland; (second row) two Quinney's, Cora Desbon (in white) and Abbie Pinkham Fletcher, and in back of them, Ernest Fletcher, D. Simmons, Eugene Perry (big hat), and Herbert Stone, with hands in pocket; (against building:) unknown, ? Wakefield, Ben Jennison, Addie Fletcher Smith, and Evie Tanner; (on other side of teacher) Abbie Grant Maling, Ana Stone, Angie Wildes, Fannie Stone (pigtails), and ? Twombly; (in window at left) Julia Wakefield, and Callie Huff Nunan; (in window at right) Nellie Huff Parker, and Clara Pinkham Stone; (in doorway) Helena Hutchins Langsford and teacher Lauraette Hutchins Perkins. This photo was taken in the summer of 1872 by Wallace Huff. (Fred & Harriett Eaton)

PRIMARY CLASS. Teacher Helen Ward stands with her class at Cape Porpoise at the turn of the century. Sitting, from left to right, are: (front row) Millie Hutchins, Allie Moody, Robert Cluff, Walter Perkins, Frank Hutchins, Charlie Stone, George Seavey, and George Emmons; (second row) Goldie Perry, Gladys Perry, Ruby Huff, Florence Potter, Ruth Jennison, Earl Stone, Carl Stone, Pearl Nunan, and Lettie Lapierre; (back row) George Nunan, Harold Cluff, George Ridlon, Eddie Nunan, Laura Conley, Edna Fletcher, Emma Brooks, Cassie McKenney, Bessie Nunan, and Mildred Nunan. (Huff Family)

CEMETERY. To the left of the Charles Heber Clough house (at right) is Arundel Cemetery at the turn of the century. In the early 1890s, Bass Cove Cemetery on North Street was the oldest and only town burial ground and it was fast running out of room. In 1893 it was voted to spend $450 for 10 acres owned by C.H. Pope in the Town House area at Seven Corners. The new cemetery would be called "Arundel" and Charles Clough, living right next door and unmarried, agreed to be the caretaker. Townspeople also rallied around and the first fifty stockholders were sold lots for $15, location to be decided by a draw. Many of the lots were immediately filled by those moved from family graveyards. Since then trees have been planted, granite posts and an iron gate erected, and more land annexed. Arundel Cemetery, one of seventy-one in Kennebunkport, has the distinction of being chosen by former President and Mrs. George H. Bush as their final resting place. (Luverne Clough Preble)

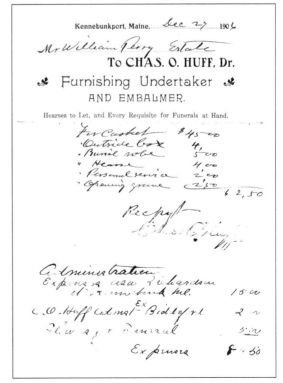

UNDERTAKER BILL. (Huff Family)

CLOCK FARM. A landmark on the corner of Goose Rocks Road and Route 9, the Clock Farm has been in the Emmons' family since 1892 when it was purchased by Grosvenor B. Emmons from his boyhood friend Peter Johnson. The original clock and tower were taken from a factory owned by "Gros" Emmons in Laurence, Mass. It seems while Mr. Emmons was away on a business trip, his employees banded together and raised $250 to present him with a Howard clock upon his return. Mr. Emmons had a tower built on the factory roof to hold the clock but there was so much squabbling about who had the correct time — the clock or the workers — that he had the tower and clock taken down and moved to his recently purchased summer farm in Kennebunkport. When the Howard Clock Co. workers came to install the clock in its new location, they convinced the owner that he should invest in a newer, better clock, for only $1000. That is the clock that is there today. The main building of the farm dates to 1773. (Emmons Family)

SERVANTS' COTTAGE. Employees who helped tend the horses and maintain the Clock Farm were housed in this smaller, dormered building called the "servants' quarters." It was destroyed in the 1947 forest fires. The Clock Farm itself was saved from the fires by a fast-thinking neighbor who started a bonfire, causing a backdraft that diverted the blaze. (Emmons Family)

EMMONS FAMILY. The first of the Emmonses to own the Clock Farm were, from left to right: (seated) Grosvenor Butterick Emmons, daughter Helen Mildred, and wife Frances Ellen Sims; (standing) sons Herbert Irving and Harry Grosvenor. George Harry Emmons, the present owner, is the son of Harry Grosvenor who attended school on the Biddeford Pool Road. (Emmons Family)

ALL ABOARD. Drivers and their teams (as horse and carriages were called) line up at the Dock Square trolley station, ready to transport passengers to their final destinations. In 1900 the first mail was delivered by trolley to Cape Porpoise; also in that year, the Sanford and Cape Porpoise Railway began construction of the Casino, a large dance hall with two dining rooms on Bickford Island, which attracted many more visitors to the Cape and proved a lucrative addition to the railway. With shipbuilding on the wane, the electric railway ushered in the new era of tourism, a main attraction through the present day. Many old trolley cars are on display at the Seashore Trolley Museum on the Log Cabin Road. (Huff Family)

Two

1900–1909

TOWN HOUSE JUNCTION. Trolley passengers could make connections to Kennebunk and Sanford from this busy station in 1901. A ticket to Dock Square was $.05. (Kenneth Hutchins Family)

LOUISE EMMONS. Daughter of Orlando and Fannie Ghen Emmons, this photogenic little girl attended the Town House school in the early 1900s. (Huff Family)

"OLDEST LADY IN TOWN. Mrs. Ruth Curtis, born Dec. 11, 1798, married Jacob Curtis and had a child while living in Kennebunkport, named Hannah, who married a Huff. Mrs. Curtis was the daughter of Shadrach Fairfield. Mrs. Curtis lived to be 103 years old" (from *The Biddeford Daily Record*, Dec. 11, 1901). Ruth Curtis lived in three centuries. (Huff Family)

WHAT FUN. Sisters Dorothy and Nancy Walker set out for their afternoon carriage ride over the dirt road bordering the Walker estate off Ocean Avenue. The Walker family spent summers at the estate they had built in 1901, the year Dorothy was born. Dorothy was to become the mother of U.S. President George Bush, who vacations at the estate. (George Bush Family album)

DAPPER SAILORS. Note the wicker chairs in this water craft with passengers George Herbert Walker (left) and Mr. Potter, a family member. (George Bush Family album)

TIDAL POOL. Cooling off on a warm summer day at the Walker estate are, from left to right: friend Betty Trotter, Nancy Walker, and Dorothy Walker. (George Bush Family album)

ON THE ROCKS. Members of the Walker party enjoy a fishing holiday in Kennebunkport in the early 1900s. From left to right are: (standing) Dorothy Walker, Mr. Potter, an unidentified man with his back to the camera and, to the far right, George Herbert Walker, Dorothy's father; (seated) Mrs. Mildred Wear Kotany with Nancy. Mrs. Kotany, an aunt to the six Walker children, was affectionately known as "Tonta." (George Bush Family album)

PHOTOGENIC. Nancy Walker, in turn-of-the-century bathing attire, wades in the shallow water off Walker's Point. Nancy, less than two years older than her sister Dorothy, is a namesake to George Bush's sister, Nancy Ellis. (George Bush Family album)

PLAYMATES. Sunshine, water, and rocks to climb — an idyllic setting for four little girls at the turn of the century. From left to right are: a friend, Nancy Walker, Dorothy Walker, and Betty Trotter at Walker's Point. (George Bush Family album)

AT CLEAVES COVE. Safroni Cleaves stands in the doorway of the family home at Cleaves Cove, beyond the Bush estate off Ocean Avenue, going toward Cape Porpoise. Perhaps the young vacationers pictured stopped at the cove to pick strawberries which grew in abundance, c. 1900. (Rimmer Family)

THE BOAT CLUB.
Located on Ocean Avenue,
the "clubhouse" was built
in 1888 in conjunction
with the founding of the
Kennebunkport River
Club. It was from here that
"Carnival Night" originated
— the last hurrah of summer
in which a carnival of
decorated boats paraded
up the Kennebunk River.
(George Bush Family album)

RIVER CARNIVAL. In this c. 1900 photograph, gaily decorated canoes and floats, colored lanterns, and music set the stage for the annual carnival held by the River Club on the Kennebunk River. (Kenneth Hutchins Family)

CAPE SQUARE. A watering trough stands in the center of town and remained there until the 1920s when an errant motorist hastened its demise. S.H. Pinkham's Store can be seen at the end of the Pier Road. The vacant lot at left "where the square and Mills Road meet," is now home to the Wayfairer restaurant and is the subject of the poem below, based on a tale originating in the early 1800s (also see page 33). (Carolyn Craig)

THE HALIBUT POND

You've heard of Mellen's and Mary Ann's,
And maybe the Mill Pond, too.
Tradition tells of another pond,
Those earlier settlers knew.

Nearer than these was Halibut Pond
Where the Square and Mills Road meet;
Only a pond when the tide came in,
With minnows so oft replete.

Not far away was the old town pump,
A need in those days of yore;
With the wat'ring trough, a hollowed log,
Close by Uncle Stephen's door.

They tell this tale of Halibut Pond -
A pedler of fish there came.
One Saturday night with surplus stock,
And no one his zeal could blame.

So into the pond he placed the fish
For safety till Monday morn,
But alas for him, the tide went out,
As it comes and then is gone.

For high and dry on that bit of marsh,
Had been left his stock in trade.
What wonder that Monday morning there
Found a fisherman dismayed.

The tide comes in, and the tide recedes,
And the roads wind on their way;
While the pond that never was, is gone,
the tale of a by-gone day.

(by Helen Ward Nunan)

SAILING. Family recreation was at the water's edge for these young people at home on the Kennebunk River, c. 1910. (Kenneth Hutchins Family)

PADDY CREEK. It's clear sailing to the Cape Porpoise pier and beyond for these youngsters, c. 1900. They are, from left to right: Al Seavey, Alton Perkins, Byron Perkins, George Seavey (with hat), and Stanley Perkins. (Harrison Seavey)

UNUSUAL DECOR. The jaw bones of a whale washed ashore were used to surround this lawn decoration at the Allen's summer cottage at Cape Porpoise, c. 1900. (Huff Family)

SEAVEY HOMESTEAD. George F. Seavey and family lived here at Paddy Creek in Cape Porpoise at the turn of the century. The home was destroyed in the fires of 1947. (Harrison Seavey)

NELSON HOUSE. Louis Nelson, Alta Nelson, and Luther Emerson at the Nelson home on the Langsford Road, *c.* 1908. The barn was moved from the Mills Road and later torn down. Luther Emerson owned the Prospect House at the foot of Crow Hill. (Janet Huff Lombard)

PIER ROAD. Nelson's barn can be seen from across the Cove at Henry Hutchins's fishhouse. (Kenneth Hutchins Family)

CAPE SQUARE SCHOOL. The plaque over the schoolhouse door reads "School District #3 1893." The school was torn down in 1925 and students transferred to the new school on the Mills Road. (Kenneth Hutchins Family)

CLASS of 1903. Classmates at the Cape in 1903 are, from left to right: (front) George Emmons, Leon Ridlon, George Whitmore, Ernest Nunan, Carl Jennison, Clarence Moody, Charles Stone, and Melvin Hutchins; (second row) Marion Emmons, Violia McKenney, Maizie McKenney, Earl Stone, Carl Stone, George Emmons, William Sinnett, and Arthur Sinnett; (third row) George Nunan, Florence Potter, Gladys Perry, Nellie Emmons, Laura Conley, Mildred Nunan, Ruth Jennison, and Pearl Hutchins. (Carolyn Craig)

TOWN HOUSE SCHOOL. A potbellied stove helped take off the chill in the early 1900s at this school located on the present site of the Kennebunkport Historical Society. (Bunty Lush)

CAPE SCHOOL. Attending school in the square in the early 1900s are, from left to right: (front) Robert Cluff, Charlie Stone, Goldie Perry, Gladys Perry, Mildred Nunan, and George Nunan; (second row) Lyman H. Huff, George Seavey, Frank Hutchins, Mame Card, Lettie Lapierre, Walter Perkins, Albert Moody, and Earl Stone; (third row) Frank Fisher, Harold Cluff, Edward Stone, Edward Nunan, Ruth Jennison, Ethan Milliken, Florence Potter, Flossie Curtis, Ernestine Baston, and Bessie Nunan; (fourth row) Cassie McKinney and Edna Fletcher. (Janet Huff Lombard)

HIGH SCHOOL. The Class of 1909 included, from left to right: (front) Elizabeth Sawyer, teacher Roxie Smith, Elizabeth Rowe, Helen Seavey, Annie Goodrich, Grace Benson Thirkell, Agnis Earle, Helen Seavey, Celia Martin, Ruth Jennison, and Elizabeth Dow; (second row) ? Griffin, Ralph Derby, George Seavey, Laurence Ross, Ralph Pillsbury, and Henry Twombley; (third row) Clara Dow, Flora Smith, Hazel Clough, Eva Bonney, Mae Mitchell, Mildred Nunan, Ruby Chappell, Ruth Welsh, and Marion Maling, teacher; (fourth row) Goldie Perry, Isabelle Russell, Ruth Cluff, Ada Seavey, Ernest Nunan, Clifford Rand, and Mr. Rand, teacher; (back row) unknown, Ray Eldridge, Stanley Thirkell, Ernest Monroe, James McCabe, Bob Maling, and Clifford Wildes. Weekly wages for teachers averaged under $10. (Huff Family)

In the Town Report of 1909/10, E.L. Rand, superintendent of schools, wrote: "A High school certainly fills an important place in a small community. . . . it keeps the boys and girls at home, a very important matter. . . . In order to make our High school a thoroughly good High school, and in order that the pupils themselves may get the full benefit of their studies, they should be sent to school regularly. There is a tendency for them to stay out too often and I look to the parents to help me remedy this evil."

MOTHER AND DAUGHTER. Caroline Huff Nunan of Cape Porpoise and her daughter, Daisy, in the early 1900s. (Huff Family)

BENCHMARK. At home on the Langsford Road, Cape Porpoise, are, from left to right: Payson Huff, his wife Caroline, daughter Nell (who moved to Cuba), Daisy Nunan, Ed Huff, and a boarder, c. 1900. The Payson Huff house was the first built on the Langsford Road in the early 1850s. (Fred & Harriett Eaton)

FRIENDS. Ruby Huff, Goldie Perry, and Pearl Nunan enjoy an outing at the Cape's Wildes District, *c.* 1908. (Huff Family)

NUNANS AND HUFFS. This family group resided at the Cape at the turn of the century. In the front is Mable and Doug Huff, while at the back are Caroline, Wesley, Elisha, and Daisy Nunan. (Fred & Harriett Eaton)

CASINO WORKERS. Crowds flocking to the new dancehall and restaurant on Bickford Island meant jobs for local residents in the early 1900s. From left to right are: (front) Mary Gridley, Sylvia Nunan Wakefield, unknown, and William Sawyer, manager; (second row) Annie Wagner, Vira Cluff, Lettina Ghen Perry, and Bessie Shepard; (third row) Nellie Hutchins Eaton, unknown, Annie Hutchins Ford, unknown, and Martha Averill Walker; (back row) Maude Hutchins Hilton, Ober A. White, Charlotte White Huff, and Inez Seavey Jennison. (Huff Family)

Cape Porpoise Casino

Served to Order

CHOWDERS

Clam Chowder 15c   Fish Chowder 15c

Lobster Stew 20c
With Pickles

CLAMS

Steamed Clams with Drawn Butter 25c
Fried Clams 25c

FISH

Fried Fish 25c   Fried Cunners 25c

LOBSTERS

Plain Lobster 40c   Lobster Salad 40c   Broiled Live 65c
3o minutes required to cook Broiled Live

POTATOES

French Fried Potatoes 15c   Fresh Potato Chips 10c
Bread served with each order

———

Ice Cream 10c   Sponge Cake 5c
Tea 10c   Coffee 10c

MENU. The Casino was famous for its Shore Dinner at $.50. (Seashore Trolley Museum)

SECOND GENERATION. On the porch of the Casino are daughters of some of the first employees. From left to right are Sylvia Nunan, Evelyn Cluff, and Goldie Perry, *c*. 1910. (Huff Family)

DANCE CARD. Live orchestras drew large crowds to the Casino. But on Labor Day weekend in 1915, the Casino burned down. Because of the railway's financial difficulties, coinciding with the popularity of the automobile, the Casino was never rebuilt. (Huff Family)

Conductors' and Motormen's Ball,
CAPE PORPOISE CASINO,
Saturday Evening, Sept 19th.
FLOOR DIRECTOR—W. NASON.
AIDS: G. F. Ferguson, W. T. Flint, W. H. Bryant
W. Thibodeau. W. B. Sawyer, H. Ferguson.

ORDER OF DANCES.

Round Dancing from 8 to 9.
Promenade and Waltz.

1	Waltz
2	Schottische
3	Two Step
4	Quadrille, Lanciers
5	Waltz
6	Caprice
7	Contra, Boston Fancy
8	Waltz
9	Quadrille
10	Oxford Minuet
11	Waltz
12	Two Step
13	Contra, Portland Fancy
14	Schottische
15	Quadrille, Lanciers
16	Waltz

No Dancing Outside of the Sets.

MUSIC BY SMITH'S ORCHESTRA.

IT'S A PARTY. In this *c.* 1903 photograph, it was Betty Sawyer's birthday and her friends and family turned out to help her celebrate. From left to right are: (front) Nelson Hall, Doris Ward, Betty, unknown and unknown; (second row) Pauline Benson, Charles Emery, Thompson Norton, Howard Martin, Ernest Benson, and Minton Montgomery; (third row) unknown, Ruth Emery, Louise Tuman, Eulalie Benson, and Chadbourne Ward. (Cecil Benson)

DUCKY. Fannie Ghen Emmons of Cape Porpoise (1868-1920) with daughter Louise (1900-1954) and feathered friend. (Huff Family)

WHERE THE BOYS ARE. Neighborhood boys from the Wildes District gather on the steps of George and Mary Etta Seavey's home overlooking Paddy Creek. From left to right are: Willis McKay, ? Sexton, Franklin Ridlon, Foster "Johnnie" Thompson, and Bert McKay. (Harrison Seavey)

SUMMER 1905. Walter Huff and Millie Sykes sail at Cape Porpoise Harbor prior to their marriage in 1912. (Huff Family)

THE *ELIZABETH B.* Captain Frank Nunan's fishing schooner, the *Elizabeth B. Nunan*, seen anchored at Cape Porpoise Harbor, *c.* 1908. It was one of the first in the area to be fitted with a gas engine, following the lead of Captain Merton Hutchins. Calvin Bryant was hired to sail with the *Elizabeth B.* crew and teach the engine's operation. (Carolyn Craig)

CREW. Captain Frank Nunan (front center with his hands in his pockets) is shown with his crew aboard the *Elizibeth B. Nunan*. Frank is the son of Richard J. Nunan who captained the first schooner in the famed Nunan Fleet which eventually consisted of more than a dozen vessels. It was the largest fleet to sail from Cape Porpoise in the late 1800s and into the next century, attracting new townspeople and boosting the local economy. As for wages, a 1905 newspaper considered it newsworthy enough to report that the crew of the *Sadie M. Nunan* had shared $32 the previous week. (Carolyn Craig)

Three

1910–1919

TRIO. Fishhouses and the Cape shoreline provide the background for this *c.* 1910 scene. On the wheelbarrow, from left to right, are: Florence Potter, Ruby Huff, and her brother William A. Perry. (Huff Family)

ALBERTA REDMOND. Alberta Cassidy Redmond, shown about 1910, arrived in Cape Porpoise from Massachusetts in the early 1930s and, as her five children grew, became an active participant in the community. She was a founding member of the American Legion Auxiliary and a staunch defender of the American flag at a time when the flag was being misused in protest of the Vietnam war. A flag was later dedicated in her memory at the Kennebunk Nursing Home where she died in 1988 at age 102. (Beryl Bilderback)

BEACH SCENE. Bathers frolic at Kennebunk Beach in this picture perfect c. 1910 post card scene looking toward the Kennebunkport shoreline. (Huff Collection)

GET TOGETHER. This gathering of well-dressed young folks provides a glimpse of what was fashionable around 1910. (Huff Family)

GOOCH'S BEACH. The bathhouses at Gooch's Beach, Kennebunk, and the Kennebunkport shoreline are visible in this early post card scene. (Kenneth Hutchins Family)

QUIET CORNER. How different the turn on Ocean Avenue looks today compared to this scene in the early 1900s. (Kenneth Hutchins Family)

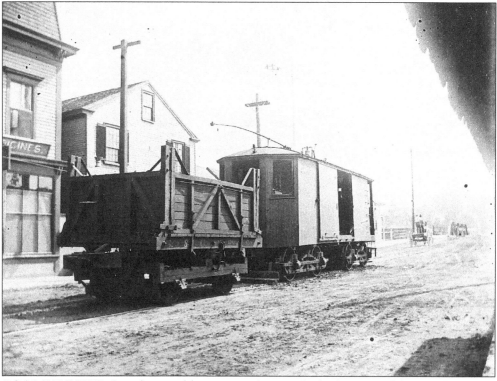

COAL DELIVERY. A coal car and boxcar travel on tracks leading to and from Perkins Coal Wharf on the Kennebunk River in the early 1900s. (Kenneth Hutchins Family)

PHOTO CONTEST. Eulalie M. Benson of Kennebunkport displays the profile that won her a spot on the pages of the *Boston Post*, *c.* 1912. Eulalie was murdered in 1961 during an attempted robbery of McKenney's, a small grocery store in the Town House area, owned by Eulalie and her husband George. (Cecil Benson)

BENSON FAMILY. Picnicking on Trott's Island off Cape Porpoise *c.* 1910 are, from left to right: (front) Ivory Ross holding Betty Gould, Florence Benson Ross, Cecil Benson, Rodney Benson, Philip and Mary Murch Benson, and Ernest Benson; (second row) Lillian Ross Wakefield, Varian Benson Dill, and Ernest Benson Jr.; (in back) Eulalie Benson McKenney, Norman Ross, and Pauline Benson Bibber. (Cecil Benson)

LANGSFORD HOUSE. Located on what was originally Huff's Neck at the end of the Langsford Road, Cape Porpoise, the Langsford House offered employment to several generations of area residents. The main house, built in 1883 and later enlarged, accommodated 150 guests and provided bathing and boating at its shores. Private residences now occupy the site. (Bunty Lush)

SUMMER HELP. Working at the Langsford House around 1910 were, from left to right: (front) Flossie Hutchins, Goldie Perry, Alex Grenwood, Irene Verrill, and Lettie Lapierre; (back) Edmond Perkins, Grace Smith Perkins, Martha Avery, Evelyn Perry, Alice Durand, Nettie Doane, Mrs. Barter, Gertrude Doane, Gladys Perry, Ruth Jennison, and Ruby Huff. (Huff Family)

ALBERT CHISHOLM. A familiar face in the Kennebunkport area in the early 1900s, Albert Chisholm heads toward Ocean Avenue. (Kenneth Hutchins Family)

WARD ROAD. Nin Avery, a farmer who lived on Springer's Hill (now the Old Cape Road) makes his rounds delivering vegetables at the Cape in the early 1900s. In the background is the Hartley Huff house on the Ward Road, now the home of Don and Joyce Huff and family. (Huff Family)

WEDDING. Fannie Coy, center, became the bride of Albert Wilbur Seavey in November 1913 at the home of her brother-in-law, J. Frank Seavey of Cape Porpoise. Attending the bride, from left to right, are: Grace Seavey Perkins, Edna Benson Seavey, Betty Churchill, Alice Whitehead Seavey, and Emma Seavey Talbot. (Harrison Seavey)

IS IT A BIRD? They all went fishing back in 1912 and look what they caught. Albert E. Hutchins, left, holds a lobster, while Herb Maier of Boston, far right, displays what looks like a bird. Or is it a hake? Also on board, at left, are Harrison Hutchins and Keith Hutchins, with the gun. (Kenneth Hutchins Family)

LOOKALIKES.

Top left: GRANDMOTHER.
Lettina Ghen Perry (1870–1962).

Top right: DAUGHTER. Gladys Perry Towne
(1895–present).

Bottom right: GRANDDAUGHTER/NIECE.
Helen Huff Holmberg (1922–1968).

UNSCHEDULED LANDING. A bi-plane headed for Portland in 1912 drew a goodly crowd when it developed engine trouble and ended up near the Arundel Cemetery. It took off safely the next day. (Cecil Benson)

BREAKWATER COURT. Following the fire in 1902 which destroyed the Ocean Bluff, the site remained vacant until 1914 when Ruel Norton built Breakwater Court. In 1948 the hotel was sold to George Boughton and renamed the Colony. Today it is owned and operated by George Boughton's daughter Jestena. (Huff Family)

TROLLEY ROUTE. Tracks in the foreground run across Route 9 at the Cape, looking toward Crow Hill and the Mansard-roof house of the Bryants, c. 1916. The house is now owned by Carolyn Bryant Craig. After the Casino fire in 1915, lack of passengers eventually forced the electric railway to end its run to Bickford Island. (Huff Family)

SUMMER 1917. Enjoying a summer day at Cape Porpoise are, from left to right: (front) Nellie Hutchins Eaton, an unidentified child, and Alec Greenwood; (back) Nettie Perry, Duffy Hutchins, and Gertrude Perry. (Fred & Harriett Eaton)

SUMMER 1919. L. Clifford Maling and Louise Emmons at a cottage around the time of their marriage. (Bunty Lush)

END OF AN ERA. A crowd gathers in 1918 on the Kennebunk River to watch the launching of the *Charles B. Wiggin* from Ward's Boatyard on the Kennebunk side. The launching of the *Kennebunk* later that year signalled the end of the flourishing shipbuilding industry on the Kennebunk, which had been in high gear since the mid-1800s. The quality of the vessels built there during that time were world renowned, due to the skills of such master boatbuilders as David Clark, W.H. Crawford, George Clark, and Charles Ward. Blame for the failing industry is directed both at an exhaused supply of local timber and the greater harbor depth needed for the newer and larger ships. But as boatbuilding declined, another industry was born–tourism. (Cecil Benson)

64

EMERY H. HUFF (1914-1993). Born on the Langsford Road, Cape Porpoise, to Lyman and Goldie Huff, Emery was valedictorian of his 1933 high school class. He was appointed to the Naval Academy in 1934 and served as a naval officer in the Pacific during World War II, attaining the rank of commander. He returned to the Cape after retiring from the navy. Interesting that, in such a small town, a contemporary and neighbor, Roger Hutchins, was also a naval officer, serving in World War II. (Huff Family)

LETTIE LAPIERRE. A Cape resident, Lettie grew up on the Langsford Road in the house built by her father, William, in 1906. She moved to the Port after her marriage to Lonnie Towne, part owner of the Towne Clark Store there. (Huff Family)

GOAT ISLAND LIGHT. George and Mary Wakefield leave the Pier at Cape Porpoise for their home at Goat Island Light, c. 1919. After many a wreck off this rocky coast, a small house and lighted tower was built on Goat Island in 1935, its beacon warning sailors of the hazardous shoreline and of the narrow entrance to the harbor. Captain John Lord of Kennebunk was the first keeper of the light and, in 1866, George Wakefield became the tenth lighthouse keeper. By that time, a new house had been built, along with a long hall providing a covered passageway to the light itself which had to be filled regularly with oil, and later with kerosene. George and Mary (Tuman) Wakefield raised four children on Goat Island: Frank, Daisy, Ethel, and John. Granddaughter Elizabeth Meserve has fond memories of summers spent on the island with her grandparents, and of the summer she worked at the Langsford House and invited fellow workers out to the island where they danced on the gleaming wood floors of the "hall." The long hall is gone now, a victim of the mighty ocean, and lighthouse keepers are only memories of days gone by. Goat Island Light, was one of the last manned lighthouses in the nation. George Wakefield was the longest serving lighthouse keeper at Goat Island, 1887-1921. (Elizabeth Meserve)

Four

1920–1929

DOUGHNUT GANG. These young entrepreneurs served doughnuts to trolley passengers and crews coming and going from the Town House station, c. 1920. From left to right are: unknown, Arthur Clough, Grace Leach, Walter Drown, Charles Andrews, Franklin Leach, Maurice "Buster" Cluff, Burton Clough, and Atwood Merrill. (Luverne Clough Preble)

ARTISTS . A summer colony of artists flourished in the Kennebunkport area during the 1800s and into the 1940s. They filled the guest houses and were ever present along the shores of Cape Arundel with their easels and paints. Here a group sets up by Victor Hutchins's fishhouse on the Langsford Road, Cape Porpoise, in the 1920s. (Fred & Harriett Eaton)

FORE AND AFT. Ardelle Eaton (left) and Roger Hutchins (right) take twins Prudence and Gordon Hutchins for a boat ride by their homes on the Langsford Road, Cape Porpoise, in the mid-1920s. (Fred & Harriett Eaton)

SUMMER GENTRY. Robert Farquhar, typical of the summer tourist in the 1920s and '30s, spent the season at the home he had built on the Langsford Road, Cape Porpoise. It was not uncommon in the early 1900s for families to "summer" at resorts such as the Langsford House or the Nonantum, returning year after year. (Huff Family)

HUTCHINSES. Albert E. Hutchins, a descendant of one of the area's earliest families, and his wife, Cora Belle Wildes, raised their family in the Wildes District, *c.* 1920. (Kenneth Hutchins Family)

GILL NETTING. A new way of fishing, known as gill netting, was introduced in the early 1900s, with Hartley Huff in the forefront. Here Ed Perkins (left) and Charles McKay are aboard Hartley's boat, the *Ethel S*, *c.* 1920. (Huff Family)

TOWN HOUSE. Buildings literally come and go in many of Maine's small towns, and Kennebunkport is no exception. This pillared structure, shown here in the 1920s at Seven Corners, was built around 1902 as the town meeting place, or Town House, as the area is still called. In later years the building also served as the local gymnasium for high school basketball games. To the right is the home for the indigent known as the Poor Farm. The Town House building was moved in 1953 to its present location on North Street where it housed the now defunct Arundel Opera Company. Today it is St. Martha's Church. (Harrison & Eleanor Seavey)

RECITAL. Ina Stanley (back row, second from left) gathers her piano students on the lawn of the South Congregational Church in the early 1920s. The Parker House is in the background. (Harrison Seavey)

ICE RUNNER. Ernest Benson and horse "Buster H" take time out from racing on a pond off Western Avenue in Kennebunk's Lower Village. Members of the driving club flooded the area with water each winter and held races Saturday mornings in the 1920s. (Cecil Benson)

CHEERY HELPERS CLUB. "Aunt Jennie" Ridlon (as she was known to the Cape's young folk) organized this group into a club known as the Cheery Helpers. They met regularly at her home on Crow Hill, c. 1920. (Harrison Seavey)

CHAMPS. Members of the Kennebunkport High School basketball team in 1926 were, from left to right:: (front) Richard Hanson, Frank Craig, Lindsey Whitcher, Carroll Snow, and Arthur Thompson; (back) James Smith, Coach Alonzo Towne, Norman Hoff, and Wilson Seavey. (Carolyn Craig)

MAINE STREET. Mail carrier Stanley Brown, seldom seen without his pipe, tends his garden off Maine Street at the Port looking toward what now is Towne Street. The buildings on the left belonged to Cliff Maling; to the right is the Welch house, c. 1920. (Priscilla Brown Martin)

ALBERT CLOUGH. Not everyone owned a car in the 1920s, so Albert Clough of the Town House area was a man to be envied in this Model-T. Born in 1877, Albert was a master carpenter and designed and built many of the fine homes on Ocean Avenue. (Luverne Clough Preble)

ICE MAN COMETH. The ice man was a familiar sight in the 1920s and, on hot summer days, not without a following of children hoping to grab an ice chip from the back of the truck. Here, a driver with Citizens Ice Co., owned by J. Frank Seavey of Cape Porpoise, makes his rounds. In summer months the company ran four trucks a day. (Harrison Seavey)

RESIDENCE SERVICE

MONTHLY BASE RATES

Unlimited Service — within the exchange service area.**

1–Party Line	— $2.75
2–Party Line	— $2.25
4–5–6–Party Line	— $2.00
Rural 15 or more — $1.75*	
Party Line	

* Rate includes wall set type of instrument ONLY — desk stand 8 cents additional per month.

TELEPHONE RATES, 1925.

PARADE. Marchers parade by Leach's store in Dock Square in the 1920s. The telephone company was across the square on the second floor where the Satellite Grill is today. (Cecil Benson)

CHURCH ON THE CAPE. In 1856, with $400 borrowed from James Huff, construction began on the Methodist Church. It was completed the following year, at a cost of $1500. The steeple, clock, stained-glass windows, and bell were added as the years went by. To the right of the church in the early 1920s was Nunan's store. The schoolhouse can be seen in the square. On the left were the Albert and Ward homes. (Harrison Seavey)

74

DUCK HUNTER. Wallace Brooks of Turbat's Creek, an avid duck hunter, shows off the "bird in the hand," c. 1920. (Kenneth Hutchins Family)

BENSON BIKER. Robert Benson rides his tricycle in the mid-1920s at the family home on West Street. The son of Ernest and May Benson, Robert was drafted into the Army Air Corp. in World War II and killed in a bombing raid in Formosa. (Cecil Benson)

ROOM FOR TWO. A motorcycle with sidecar provided transportation for Ray Hull of the Town House, c. 1920. (Luverne Clough Preble)

FERRY. Walter Shuffleburg, from the Wildes District, pulls ashore with a small boat used to ferry people across the Kennebunk River, *c.* 1920. (Kenneth Hutchins Family)

GOLF COURSE. The Cape Arundel Golf Course, located on the Kennebunk River since 1897, is a favorite of visitors and townspeople alike. The picturesque course was scientifically redesigned in the 1920s by noted Australian golfer and engineer, Walter Travis, who was much in demand throughout the country for his golf course designs. (Arundel Golf Club Collection)

UP A TREE. Dot Baker at her home on the Pier Road in the late 1920s. She and her sister Ruth grew up at the Cape. Both later moved out of state, and Dot went to California. (Huff Family)

CAMP FIRE GIRLS. At an Old Orchard Beach outing in the 1920s are, from left to right: Irma Bowley, Vera Sanborn, Betty Perkins, Marion Jennison, Ruth Bowley, and Ruth Rodick. Carolyn Craig was the group leader. (Carolyn Craig)

PAYSON T. HUFF. Noted sea captain and fisherman at the turn of the century, Payson Huff (with unidentified child) was "Uncle Payson" to most townsfolk. Son of Clement Huff, Payson also was known for his remedies and the "aroma" from his medicinal supplements extracted from cod livers. Upon celebrating his fiftieth wedding anniversary in 1905 at the age of 74, it was reported that he and his wife Caroline "are remarkably well preserved for their years." In 1920 Payson was listed as the oldest resident of Cape Porpoise. (Fred & Harriett Eaton)

BEACHCOMBERS. Three generations enjoy one of the area's favorite pastimes, a walk on the beach, c. 1926. From left to right are: Goldie Perry Huff with her children Helen and Emery, and her parents Pharaoh H. and Lettina Perry, all of Cape Porpoise. (Huff Family)

HYDRANT PERCH. Polly Seavey Johnson, now age 73, leaps a fire hydrant in front of the Seavey homestead in the Wildes District in the late 1920s. (Harrison Seavey)

Five

1930–1939

MEMORIAL DAY 1930. Marchers parade by the Soldier's Monument in the center of Dock Square. The monument, first suggested by artist Albert Graves, was dedicated in 1909 to the men and women who fought and died for their country. (Kenneth Hutchins Family)

DOCK SQUARE. Looking toward the draw bridge that takes you into Kennebunk's Lower Village, the First National Store is on the left and Benson's Snack Bar across the street where, in the early 1930s, $.55 would buy you a quart of fried clams and a hamburger. On the far right, overlooking the river, is a "Norman Rockwell-type" ice cream parlor: round, glass-top tables with matching high-back, wrought iron chairs could be found within, along with tall strawberry ice cream sodas with straws to share. (Cecil Benson)

DOWNTOWN. The Lyric Theater was the first building on the right after the bridge going into Kennebunkport in the 1930s. (Priscilla Brown Martin)

PHARMACY. In front of Miller's Drug Store in the 1930s are, from left to right: (front) E.C. Miller, his son Frank, Frank Hackett, and Philip Sawyer. Located in Kennebunkport's Dock Square, Miller's was billed as the place "where friends meet friends." One of those "friends" surely was Dr. H.L. Prescott who also served as a selectman of Kennebunkport. During his long and distinguished career, Dr. Prescott helped many of today's "oldtimers" into the world and as a result, according to 1914 records, received that year the grand sum of $7 for "reporting births and deaths." That same year, he and Drs. Merrill and Purington also reported thirty cases of whooping cough, three cases of smallpox, and one case of typhoid fever. (Cecil Benson)

LAWN PARTY. Fairgoers gather on the parsonage lawn at Cape Porpoise in the summer of 1931. (Harrison Seavey)

THOMAS GHEN. This is the Cape Porpoise man (1838–1913) said to have dug and shucked more than three thousand clams and baited four tubs of trawl line in one day. (Huff Family)

CLAMMING. The tide's out and these diggers are hard at work on the flats off Cape Porpoise in 1931. You'll find no heavy spices, and certainly no tomatoes, in this authentic New England chowder recipe below. (Kenneth Hutchins Family)

CLAM CHOWDER

1 quart clams, washed & chopped
5 or 6 potatoes, cut in small pieces
1 onion, diced
Salt pork
Pat of butter

Fry onion in 1 or 2 slices diced salt pork.
In pot, add potatoes, clams, salt & pepper. Add enough boiling water to cover. Cook until done.
Add 1 quart milk and butter. Let set.
Bring to boil before serving.

SCHOOL PLAY. George Washington (played by Lyman Huff) was the star in this 1932 tale of the South, celebrating the end of the school year, and staged at the Casino at the Port. Helen Maling played Martha. Note the front row in blackface, common in stage productions of its day. (Cecil Benson)

CHRISTMAS 1933. Ken "Sonny" Hutchins, owner of Port Lobster on Ocean Avenue, was five years old when this photo was taken at the Hutchins's home in the Wildes District. (Kenneth Hutchins Family)

ICED IN. These fish houses at the Cape could more aptly be called ice houses, judging by the size of these frozen banks in the winter of 1933. (Huff Family)

FRIGID. Neither rain nor sleet nor a temperature reading of 22 below zero deterred these hardy fox hunters in 1933. From left to right are Ken Hutchins Sr. and Byron Johnson. (Kenneth Hutchins Family)

FOXY GENTS. Hunters display their kill in front of the Ocean Bluff Garage on Ocean Avenue. They are, from left to right: Laurin Clifford Maling, Henry Goodwin, Alonzo Towne, Edward Clark, Warren Littlefield, and Seward Eldridge. (Bunty Lush)

UNDER COVER. On a family outing at Goose Rocks Beach (also known as Beachwood) in the 1930s are, from left to right: Lyman Huff, Dot Huff, Ruby Shaeffer, and Goldie Huff. (Huff Family)

ROCKY SHORE. Benny Richardson of the Wildes District joins picnickers at Cleaves Cove in the late 1930s. From left to right are Priscilla Brown, Bunty Maling, and Virginia Littlefield. (Priscilla Brown Martin)

CLASS OF '34. Kennebunkport High School students gather in Washington, D.C., on the traditional senior class trip. From left to right are: (front) Raymond Johnson, Dorothy Huff, LeRoy Ward, Ruth Clark, Carleton Landry, and Louise Tuman, chaperon; (second row) Eddie (bus driver), Charlie Caron, Ruth Seavey, Hensy?, and Mr. Green, guide; (back) Virginia Tuman, Ruth Higgins, Elizabeth Shuffleburg, and Blanche Higgins. Class speakers at commencement exercises June 6 included Carleton Landry (president), Ruth Clark (secretary-treasurer), Blanche Higgins (valedictorian), and Ruth Seavey (salutatorian). (Dorothy Huff Porter)

SUNDAY SCHOOL. The Reverend Charles Whynot, standing in back, with his students on the steps of the Church On The Cape in the early 1930s. (Harrison Seavey)

CAPE CLASSMATES. The two-room schoolhouse on the Mills Road had one room for grades 3, 4 and 5, and another for grades 6, 7, and 8. Attending in 1935 were, from left to right: Delephine Wood, Virginia Stone, Edith Peabody, Edith Brdbury, Edna Hutchins, and Ruth Redmond; (second row) Frederick Wagon, Harrison Seavey, Frank Kinnie, Florence Jennison, Lillian Seavey, Eleanor Bradbury, Alma Foster, and Ernestine Bowley; (third row) John Seavey, Fred Eaton, Harold Wood, Gordon Hutchins, Paul Seavey, and Kenneth Perkins; (back row) Prudence Hutchins, Elizabeth Wood, Gertrude Beach, Beryl Redmond, Helen Huff, Alberta Seavey, Eleanor Seavey, and Pauline Seavey. (Harrison & Eleanor Seavey)

GO-CART. Paul, Cynthia, and Albert Seavey try out their homemade go-cart near their home in the Cape's Wildes District, c. 1933. (Harrison Seavey)

ALL IN THE FAMILY. Lettie Tibbetts, holding Connie Campbell, and Tom and Minnie Cluff (a triplet) enjoy the outdoors in a glider, a popular outdoor swing in the 1930s. (Harrison Seavey)

ATLANTIC HALL. Donald Huff, in the foreground, plays pass with an unidentified friend in front of Atlantic Hall. Built around 1915, the hall is a landmark in the Cape Square. The first floor housed the fire engines and included a kitchen and small library (still there); the second floor provided space for town meetings, fairs, and a variety of celebrations. (Huff Family)

HELEN WARD NUNAN (left). A teacher, shopkeeper, and wife of Captain Howard E. Nunan of the famed Nunan fishing fleet, Helen Ward Nunan chronicled the Cape's events and people in her published works of poetry called *Cape Ways*. She was eighty-four years old when her poems were published by The Church on the Cape as a fund-raiser for the church. (Fred & Harriett Eaton)

STOREFRONT (right). In 1909 Helen Ward Nunan bought the building once owned by Stephen Hutchins in the square at the Cape. After remodeling, with an apartment on the second floor, she turned it into a dry goods shop, enticing customers not only for her wide array of soaps and linens, but also "because it smelled so good." Subsequent owners were Carl and Lois Deinstadt and Woodrow Landry. The Wayfairer restaurant is now located there. (Fred & Harriett Eaton)

TUNA FISHING. Bob Fisher, second from right, a summer vistor from Connecticut, had the boat. Ken Hutchins Sr. of the Wildes District had the seamanship, and the two tourists on each end caught the tuna on a chartered fishing expedition out of the Port in 1937. (Kenneth Hutchins Family)

TAXI. With the appearance of the automobile, P.H. Perry of the Langsford Road, Cape Porpoise, turned his livery stable, built by Bell and Fletcher, into an "auto stable" offering minor maintenance, repair, and taxi services. In 1938 he purchased this 1928 Nash (with a new car guarantee) for $200 and a trade-in. (Huff Family)

RACERS. A handcrafted model boat awaits "the big race" from the Pier at Cape Porpoise. The races pitted fisherman against fisherman and originated in the late 1930s after boasts of "my boat's better'n your boat" got put to the test. The Model Schooner Race has recently been revived, and is sponsored by the Kennebunkport Historical Society. (Fred & Harriett Eaton)

AT BRADBURY'S. Soft drinks were $.05 and Rudy Vallee was in his prime when this photo was taken in the late 1930s of Donald Huff at Bradbury's Snack Bar in Cape Porpoise Square. (Huff Family)

RHYTHM BAND. There was no lack of musical talent at the Cape, especially from the descendants of Dana Cluff. In 1938 Murial Truman organized youngsters from the Mills Road school into a rhythm band. (Harrison & Eleanor Seavey)

BATTER UP! Seven makes a team for these Cape sluggers in the mid-1930s. From left to right are: (front) Eleanor Seavey and Prudence Hutchins; (second row) Elizabeth Wood and Gertrude Beach; (back row) Beryl Redman with Alberta and Pauline Seavey. (Harrison Seavey)

ATHLETES. Pauline McKenney (left) and Irene Monroe played basketball for Kennebunkport High School in 1938. (Kenneth Hutchins Family)

GRANDMOTHER. Annie B. Adams, wife of Frank S. Adams and grandmother to Priscilla Brown, at her home near the Clock Farm, Goose Rocks Beach, then known as Beachwood. Turn the page to see who comes to visit. (Priscilla Brown Martin)

TO GRANDMOTHER'S HOUSE. Vaness "Bunty" Maling (left) and Priscilla Brown hitched the wagon to Bunty's pony named "Chubby" and off they went from Maine Street to visit Priscilla's grandmother. In the winter, the two girls swapped the wagon for a sleigh. (Priscilla Brown Martin)

Six

1940s and Beyond

GOOSE ROCKS BEACH. To the north of Kennebunk Beach lies spectacular sand and surf known as Goose Rocks Beach, a favorite of families because of its gentle waves. It's said that the three-mile beach got its name from the many wild geese which nestled on the offshore rocks. (Emmons Family)

HOOKED. Hartley Huff uses a gaff to pull up to a larger vessel at Cape Porpoise Harbor, *c.* 1940s. Though he couldn't swim, which was not uncommon among fishermen, Hartley spent his life on the sea and is remembered with affection after his death in 1973 at the age of 88. (Fred & Harriett Eaton)

MOOSE CROSSING. The Kennebunk River is in the background of this post card scene. (Fred & Harriett Eaton)

WED 70 YEARS. Ken and Betty Hutchins of the Wildes District celebrated their seventieth wedding anniversary in 1994. They are at home here in the 1940s. (Arnold & Kay Stinson)

SWEETHEARTS. Eleanor Bradbury and Harrison Seavey, both age 16, joined their families for an outing at the Seavey camp on the Mills Road, Cape Porpoise. They celebrated their fiftieth wedding anniversary November 10, 1994. (Harrison & Eleanor Seavey)

FILL 'ER UP. Israel Maling owned and operated this City Service Garage on School Street, c. 1940. (Bunty Lush)

ROAD CREW. Taking a brief but welcome break from road building and repair is this crew headed by Clifford Maling, c. 1940. (Bunty Lush)

FOUR ACRES INN. Running boards on early automobiles had many uses, as evidenced by this group in front of the Four Acres Inn on the Mills Road, Cape Porpoise, c. 1940. From left to right are: Harrison S. Holton, Ralph Perkins, Emmie Talbot, Grace Perkins, Hannah Perkins, and Arthur Talbot. The inn was owned by Ralph and Grace Perkins. (Harrison Seavey)

KENNBUNKPORT LIBRARY. From bank to Custom House to library, this 1813 building on Maine Street was first used as a library in 1898 by Anne Talbot, who occupied the second floor above the Custom House. The Custom House moved to Portland in 1912 and local artist Abbott Graves later bought the building, donating it to the Public Kennebunkport Library Association in memory of his son. Today it is the Louis T. Graves Memorial Library. An addition was built in 1956. (Louis T. Graves Memorial Library Photo)

AUTHOR'S HOUSE. Workers pause during the construction of author Kenneth Roberts's House in the Wildes District in 1938. In the early 1930s Roberts wrote *Arundel*, the first in a series on happenings during the American Revolution. At the time of the Revolution, Arundel encompassed the Kennebunkport area, and the author incorporated local names and landmarks to relate the tale of Benedict Arnold's journey through Abenaki territory to Quebec. Roberts named his home "Seawood Cottage." (Bunty Lush)

FOUR GENERATIONS. In this family group, later to claim five generations for more than thiry years are, from left to right: Lettina Perry, Inez Ghen, Lyman Huff, Dot and Paul Porter with daughter Connie, and Goldie Huff, *c.* 1942. (Dot Huff Porter)

1942 TEAM. Members of the Kennebunkport High School basketball team from left to right were: (front) Joseph Welch, Gordon Hutchins, Gerald Goodwin, John Eldridge, and Francis Drown; (back) Cecil Benson Jr., Robert Boston, Wallace Dill, Harrison Seavey, and Warren Andrews. (Harrison Seavey)

TAKE OUT. Customers line up at Hazel Wildes's Lobster Shack at the Pier in Cape Porpoise on a summer day in the 1940s. Captain Frank Nunan first had a restaurant there named the Porpoise. (Fred & Harriett Eaton)

BEFORE. During World War II this radar observation tower was constructed by the U.S. Government on Stone Haven Hill, overlooking Cape Porpoise Harbor. (Fred & Harriett Eaton)

AFTER. Remains of the radar tower, demolished in 1949, provided fill to widen the road and build a ramp leading to the Pier at Cape Porpoise. (Fred & Harriett Eaton)

BROTHERS. Generations of families enjoyed skating on the Mill Pond at the Cape. From left to right are Emery, Lyman Jr., and Donald Huff, c. 1940. (Huff Family)

IN THE AIR CORPS. A P-47 pilot with the Army Air Corps in World War II, Donald Huff was with the Ninth Air Force bomber group flying over France on D-Day, 1944. He was killed in action over Luxembourg in 1945, just a week after his twenty-fifth birthday, and was posthumously awarded the Distinguished Flying Cross. Others lost in World War II were Byron Hoff, Kenneth Perkins, Bobby Benson, Jack McLean, Robert Warner, Richard Merrill, Richard Simmons, and Charles Rouleau. (Huff Family)

LUNCH CROWD. Bradbury's luncheon counter at the Cape was a popular gathering place in the late 1940s. From the Cape are: Connie Campbell (center), Edith Bradbury (right), and Winkie (back row, center). (Fred & Harriett Eaton)

POST OFFICE. Abby Ridlon (left) and Florence Nunan, c. 1950, worked many years at the post office on the Langsford Road, Cape Porpoise. Florence Nunan became postmistress in the early 1940s and presided there throughout the war years, when townsfolk gathered twice a day waiting for letters from loved ones in the Armed Forces to be sorted. (Fred & Harriett Eaton)

MAIL'S IN.
Ruth Thurston of
the Langsford Road
helps out at the
Cape's post office in
December 1948. (Fred
& Harriett Eaton)

SHORT WAVE. Pearl Nunan listens to the radio at her home on the Mills Road, Cape Porpoise, where she could tune in to broadcasts from the fishermen at sea, c. 1945. (Fred & Harriett Eaton)

BEFORE THE FIRE. The SOCONY (Standard Oil Company of New York) gas station and community store on King's Highway, Goose Rocks Beach, was one of many buildings at the beach lost in the devastating 1947 forest fires which ran rampant through the area. (Emmons Family)

ALL GONE. The buildings on this street leading to Goose Rocks Beach were burned to the ground in the 1947 fire, fueled by a drought and October winds. (Beryl Bilderback)

SAVED. Clarie Nickerson's house, in the background, was miraculously spared as the fires swept through the Goose Rocks area in 1947. A report in the *Biddeford Journal* lists approximately two hundred homes lost or damaged in the Kennebunkport area. Among those suffering losses: Mr. and Mrs. Donald Bryant (Crow Hill); Mrs. Leonard Dour, a two hundred-year-old-house (Goose Rocks); George W. Deinstadt, two places (Nunan's Cove Road); Willis McKay (Nunan's Cove Road, Cape Porpoise); Mrs. Dorothy Migneauly, four pieces of property (Goose Rocks Beach); Otis Nunan (Mills Road, Cape Porpoise); George Perkins, farm (Wildes District); Mrs. Isabelle Prescott (Wildwood Road, Goose Rocks Beach); Mr. and Mrs. Glendon Robert (Fisher's Lane, Cape Porpoise); Mr. and Mrs. Fred Severance (Wildes district); J Fred Smith, four houses (Goose Rocks Beach); Arthur B. Welch, greenhouse and home (Mills Road). (Beryl Bilderback)

CEREMONY. Following the fires in the fall of 1947, the area fire companies joined together in a fund-raising drive to add to or replace badly needed equipment. Enough money was raised to include the purchase of four new fire trucks and to remodel the fire hall at the Cape. On hand to accept the Cape's rewards were, from left to right: Fred, Russell, and Prentice Kitteridge (who were major players in the fund-raising effort), Wendall "Rap" Cluff, Dana Campbell, and Arnold Stinson. The name of the organization was also changed from the Atlantic Hose Company to the Atlantic Engine Company. (Fred & Harriett Eaton)

SOUTH CONGREGATONAL CHURCH. Built in 1824, the church on Temple Street has undergone many renovations over the years, including moving the sanctuary to the second floor in 1875. The first floor then became available as a meeting place, thus the name "Temple Hall." This c. 1940 photograph shows the steeple, reminiscent of a Christopher Wren design, and the portico (added in 1912). The small building to the left is no longer there. (Priscilla Brown Martin)

HONOR ROLL. Members of the newly formed American Legion Auxiliary gathered at the Meeting Place on Memorial Day 1946 at the unveiling of the veteran's Memorial Honor Roll. American Legion official Woodbury Stevens stands to the left of auxiliary members Bertha Bunnell and Mildred Cornealy (auxiliary president). (Beryl Bilderback)

POPPY SEASON. Harrison Seavey buys a poppy from Elizabeth Nunan, under the watchful eye of Alberta Redman, who was in charge of Poppy Day for the American Legion Auxiliary. Selling poppies made by veterans was a statewide fund-raiser to benefit the veterans' hospital in Togus. (Beryl Bilderback)

PORT GRADS. High school's over for Natalie Towne and Priscilla Brown, two of nine graduates of Kennebunkport High School in 1946. The Fred Snow house, Main Street, Kennebunkport, is in the background. (Priscilla Brown Martin)

HIGH SCHOOL. Grade school classes were held on the first floor and the second floor was the area high school. In 1947, when this photograph was taken, the older students were transferred to Kennebunk High School. In 1953 the younger children were sent to the new Consolidated School at the Port. Soon after, the many district schools were closed. (Bunty Lush)

112

CLASS OF '47. The last class to graduate from Kennebunkport High School is shown on their class trip in Washington, D.C. From left to right are: (front) Albert Seavey, Wayne Pierce, Norman Clough, Robert Dunton, Robert Schmidt, Donald Thuirston, Ernest Lush, and Robert Stinson; (back) Curly (bus driver), Bunty Maling, Mary Higgins, Mary Adams, Robert Wildes, Sue Wildes, Lorraine McKenna, Thelma Mosher, Jean Willey, and Paula Milekue. While in the Capitol, the class toured Admiral Byrd's ship, the *Mt. Olympus*, escorted by Naval Officer Emery Huff of Cape Porpoise. (Bunty Lush)

SARDINES. Fishermen off Cape Porpoise haul in nets full of sardines. From left to right are: Frank Holbrook, Nick Poli, Ken Holbrook Jr., Ken Sr., and Jimmy King, c.1940. (Fred & Harriett Eaton)

HOT LOBSTER. Fred Eaton cooks a surplus of lobster at his fishhouse on the Langsford Road in the 1940s. Better to be sold cooked than to appear anything less than "live and kickin'." (Fred & Harriett Eaton)

CLUFF'S STORE. The death of Dana Cluff in 1940 was a blow to the Cape fishermen who, for years, had gathered at "Cluff's" store to swap tales and play pool. But old habits die hard and for awhile they still came to the building which had been passed on to Wendell "Rap" Cluff. Among those gathered in front are, from left to right: Arnold Nickerson, Harry Brown, Nig Sinnett, Jim Ridlon, Charles Averill, and Harry Etherington. (Fred & Harriett Eaton)

FISHERMEN'S CLUB. Members of the Fishermen's Club play cards at Cluff's, *c.* 1948. Clockwise, from the head of the table, are Jimmy Ridlon, Lyman Huff, Harry Etherington, Alec Greenwood, George Nunan, WalterDienstart,and Harry Brown. (Fred & Harriett Eaton)

FAIRGOERS 1949. Albania "Dolly" Merrill, in the foreground, attends an "Old Country Store" fair in the Atlantic Hall, Cape Porpoise, sponsored by the Women's Guild. A resident of the Langsford Road, Dolly was well-known for her extensive doll collection and winter swims in the icy Atlantic. (Huff Family)

OLDTIMERS. These three gentlemen stand on the grounds of the Sinnett House, a popular summer hotel built in the 1860s on the Langsford Road, Cape Porpoise. P.H. Perry is in the middle; the other two are unidentified. (Huff Family)

THE *REGINA*. Author Booth Tarkington, a summer resident of Kennebunkport from about 1917 until his death in 1946, spent many hours writing aboard this boat on the Kennebunk River. The *Regina*, built in 1891, deteriorated after his death and in 1952 it was towed out to sea and sunk. (Bunty Lush)

BAIT SHED. A new bait shed takes shape on Governor's Wharf on the Kennebunk River, site of an early Abenaki summer settlement. On the roof are Harry "Bud" Brown and Ernest Julian, with Sonny Hutchins, Fred Cook, Albert Hatch, and Lorin Griffin below. Further down Ocean Avenue is Kings Highway (on the left), one of the oldest highways in the nation. (Kenneth Hutchins Family)

PET GULL. Even the seagulls found a friend in Winkie, shown here feeding his tamed gull. Winkie took great delight in asking others to feed the bird, knowing it wouldn't take food from anyone but him. The gull also followed him out fishing and back. Winkie was instrumental in organizing the Fishermen's Club in the 1940s. (Fred & Harriett Eaton)

WINKIE. The quintessential New England fisherman, Winkie (Elwyn) Perry was a colorful presence in the Kennebunkport area in his latter years, until his death in August 1961. Once a city boy residing in Boston and New York, he retired to the Cape and set up housekeeping in a fishhouse on the Langsford Road. If you come across a painting of a two-dormered fishing shack on the water's edge, with brightly painted lobster buoys dangling from the eaves and lobster traps piled around, it may be the "Perrywinkle," Winkie's home and fishhouse which was a favorite subject for artists. (Fred & Harriett Eaton)

STORM DAMAGE. A tangle of nets, buoys, and traps draw onlookers at Cape Porpoise in the 1940s, while the fishermen salvage what they can and figure their losses from another big storm. (Harriett & Fred Eaton)

RECOURSE. Fishermen gather in Atlantic Hall, Cape Porpoise, to await word from the Red Cross as to how much they'll be compensated for lobster traps and gear lost in a big storm. (Fred & Harriett Eaton)

DREDGING. A dredging operation deepens the Cove at Cape Porpoise in 1950, as seen from the Pier. (Fred & Harriett Eaton)

PIPED ON SHORE. Mud dredged from the Cove is piped onto the shore. (Huff Family)

PIANO MAN. Rap Cluff of Cape Porpoise (center) and two members of his band entertain at one of the local dances, c. 1950. One of Dana and Carrie Cluff's twelve children, Rap was reknowned for his musical talents, which included the ability to play several instruments and a lively honky tonk piano. He died of the flu at age forty-seven, leaving a wife and four children. (Beryl Bilderback)

PLAYHOUSE. The Kennebunkport Playhouse on the Old River Road drew nationally known entertainers to the area in the 1940s and '50s, with one such performer being singer Jane Morgan, sister of the Playhouse's owner, Bob Currier. Ms. Morgan also owned a house at the Port, which she claimed was haunted. (Huff Collection)

CAPTAIN.
Frank "Nig" Sinnett of Cape Porpoise heads out to sea aboard his fishing boat the *Rita & Olive*. The boat was built for him and Harold Day at Baum's Boatyard on the Kennebunk River. Frank suffered disfiguring facial burns as a teenager when a boat he was on exploded during refueling at the Pier. In the 1940s his quick actions help save the life of P.H. Perry, then in his mid-seventies, who had suffered a heart attack outside his home. Perry, as he was often called, lived to be ninety-three. (Fred & Harriett Eaton)

LAUNCHING —
The *Rita & Olive*, sporting a six-figure price tag, prepares to sail from Baum's Boatyard in 1952. A year later it was wrecked off Block Island. No hands were lost. (Fred & Harriett Eaton)

MACKEREL FISHING. Arnold Stinson (left) and Winkie Perry, both from Cape Porpoise, wonder what the night will bring while mackerel fishing aboard Arnold's boat, the *Kathleen*, in 1948. Mackerel fishermen went out in the evening, lowered their nets, and spent the night on the boat. In the morning they dragged in the mackerel and headed for home. Of this evening, Winkie wrote: "Nets out. Captain Arnold studys the lights on shore and wonders if our location and drift will be OK or should we have steamed another 5 or 10 minutes. Or is it going to be one of those queer nights, no air and the nets badly bungled . . . . Well, morning will tell the story and it's generally OK." The demand for mackerel in the 1940s and '50s was a boon to the fishing industry. (Fred & Harriett Eaton)

BAUM'S CREW. Herb Baum Sr. (far left) and crew take a break from the hull they're working on. From left to right are: Baum, ? Elwood, George Cooper, Lonnie Doane, Francis Clough, Greg Brannen, Lionel Emereau, Ken Campbell, and Warren Brooks. (Fred & Harriett Eaton)

NEWLYWEDS. Robert and Dot Stinson (center), now living in Melbourne, Florida, are honored at a reception at Atlantic Hall, Cape Porpoise, following their wedding in 1950. With them are Robert's parents, Arnold and Kay Stinson of the Langsford Road. (Bunty Lush)

ARNOLD STINSON.

OLDE GRIST MILL . From North Street, turn down Mill Lane and there, on the banks of the Kennebunk River, you'll find the site of one of the country's last tidal mills. Built in 1749 by Thomas Perkins III, and still owned by his descendants, the little mill went about its job of grinding corn in harmony with the tides until 1937. Its usefulness as a mill then over, it was turned into a restaurant, with its charm intact, and operated by David and Susan Lombard. From its weatherbeaten shingles and shiny wide board floors, to its elevator and original scales, the mill remained a treasured town landmark and was named to the National Register of Historic Places in 1973. On September 14, 1994, as this book was headed for publication, an early morning fire destroyed the Olde Grist Mill. Police reports indicate the fire may have been set on purpose. The loss is a tragic one, as can been seen above: on the left is the Olde Grist Mill as it once stood (Huff Family); on the right is all that remained after the fire (CPS).

Acknowledgments

The materials have been gathered; the captions have been written. The "story" has been put to bed, so to speak. Yet there remains unfinished business. Looking back over the past months of collecting materials, I'm struck by the graciousness of those who opened their homes and family albums to me. I'm also mindful that, without them, there would be no book.

Happily, for me and for others whose families and/or dwellings appear on these pages, the trust and generosity of a few have made this step back in time a reality for the many. And to these "authors" I offer my profound thanks.

Also, my special thanks to the following who went above and beyond to make my job easier and more enjoyable: Carolyn Bryant Craig, who loaned me her entire family album and told intriguing stories of the Cape's early days, including those in which she was my mother's Camp Fire Girl leader; Cecil Benson who watched with trepidation as I departed with many photos from his treasured collection—and then agreed to loan me more; Harrison Seavey, who has done extensive geneological research and who indulged me for the better part of a hot summer afternoon while I looked through his many albums and hundreds of photos, and then shared with me a family reminiscence written by his talented granddaughter; Harriett Eaton for the many "fishermen" photos taken at the Cape and contacts made on my behalf; Mary Bryant, my main source for historical data and research—all authors should have a Mary; Ann Fales of Cape Arundel Inn who looked up phone numbers and provided me with sources for many of the photos in this book. Carl Bartlett Sr. of Port Hardware—ditto; Luverne Preble for her enthusiasm for this project and for taking the time to send me a newspaper photo of my dad with the Kennebunk High School football team in 1932; Linda Wade for her generous library research; Beryl Bilderback for her support and energy in locating the "missing" photos; to all of you who greeted me with, "We're related, you know." I didn't know. And it made me feel special; to my daughters Brenda and Sandi who gave me a crash course on computers and calmed my hysteria when the screen went blank; to my ancestor, Ferdinand Huff, who settled in Cape Porpoise in the 1600s; to the Freemans, Bradburys, Perkinses, and others whose writings aided in my research; and to the Kennebunk boy and now-departed editor who shaped my thinking, dotted my i's, and got me started as a journalist—my dad, Paul Porter.

CPSIA information can be obtained
at www.ICGtesting.com
Printed in the USA
LVHW101428181220
674516LV00007B/87